The Spirit of Fatherhood

Activating the Next Generation of

Sons and Daughters

Larry L. Burden

Copyright

The Spirit of Fatherhood
by Larry L. Burden

Copyright © 2022 by Larry L. Burden

All rights reserved. This book is protected by the copyright laws of the United States of America. This book may not be copied or reprinted for commercial gain or profit. The use of short quotations or occasional page copying for personal or group study is encouraged. Permission will be granted upon request from Larry L. Burden. All rights reserved. Any emphasis added to Scripture quotations is the author's own.

Scripture quotations marked NASB are taken from the New American Standard Bible, © 1960, 1962, 1963, 1968, 1971, 1972, 1973, 1975, 1977, 1995 by the Lockman Foundation. Used by permission.

Scripture quotations marked NIV are taken from the New International Version, © 1973, 1978, 1984, 2011 by Biblica, Inc. Used by permission of Zondervan.

Scripture quotations marked AMP are taken from the Amplified Bible, © 1954, 1958, 1962, 1964, 1965, 1987 by The Lockman Foundation. Used by permission.

Scripture quotations marked MSG are taken from The Message, © 1993, 1994, 1995, 1996, 2000, 2001, 2002 by NavPress. Used by permission.

Scripture quotations marked NLT are taken from the New Living Translation, © 1996 by Tyndale House Publishers, Inc. Used by permission.

Scripture quotations marked TLB are taken from The Living Bible, © 1971 by Tyndale House Foundation. Used by permission.

Scripture quotations marked NLT are taken from the New Living Translation, © 1996 by Tyndale House Publishers, Inc. Used by permission.

Scripture quotations marked TLB are taken from The Living Bible, © 1971 by Tyndale House Foundation. Used by permission.

Scripture quotations marked TPT are taken from The Passion Translation, © 2022 BroadStreet® Publishing Group, LLC. All Rights Reserved. Used by permission.

Scripture quotations marked NKJV are taken from the New King James Version, © 1982 by Thomas Nelson, Inc. Used by permission.

What Christian Leaders Are Saying About *The Spirit of Fatherhood*

Apostle Larry Burden has birthed a timely and impactful message paving a practical pathway for spiritual sons and daughters to journey deeper into the heart of Father. His message speaks both a tender and yet urgent call to the body of Christ. Answering the call and stepping into a mature revelation of the significant role of father/mother mentors will empower Kingdom generations. We are excited to get this message into the hands of our congregation for spiritual equipping.

Pastors Pat and Bob Beaty
Cornerstone Church, Brenham, Texas

******

Many Christians approach God as an abstract force, the creator of all existence, the source of blessings and curses, the epicenter of moral standards, and the ruler of eternity. Indeed, most Christians go through life with this understanding and live upright, productive lives while meeting life's challenges the best they can.

But when they are faced with obstacles beyond their capabilities, they need something more. They need to go deeper into God, not into the *things* of God—not merely his protection, his provision, or his guidance—but into God himself. They need to reach the heart of God.

All that we know and love flows from God's heart like the river of life in Revelation 22. And the only way to approach God's heart is with our hearts; our entire beings lost in abandonment; fully immersed in his Spirit; nothing hidden, nothing held back.

In *The Spirit of Fatherhood*, Larry Burden takes us to the heart of the Father, that place from whom all blessings flow. It is a necessary journey to the headwaters of God's being to discover the transformative power that knows no bounds.

"And the leaves of the tree are for the healing of the nations" (Revelation 22:3).

Apostle Clay Nash

Author of: *Activating the Prophetic, Relational Authority— Authentic Leadership, God Dreams to Make America Great Again.*

******

From beginning to end, this book is rich with goodness and gold — rich with the pulse of our Father's heart for us. Words like this can only be penned by someone anchored in a true identity of sonship who also exemplifies apostolic fatherhood with such grace, love, and wisdom. "The Heart of Fatherhood" is an invitation to step into a greater understanding and responsibility of what it will take to shift the statistics of fatherlessness, so generations of sons and daughters flourish with heaven-touches-earth destiny.

Dana Sleger, Ph.D., Austin, Texas

******

I strongly encourage you to get *The Spirit of Fatherhood* in your hands and in your heart! Having long known Larry Burden as a friend and as an apostolic leader with a father's heart, I can tell you he is the real deal. *The Spirit of Fatherhood* is a heart level book that will speak to your heart while imparting revelatory Biblical truth! This book will give you clear definition and practical application of what spiritual sons and daughters are, what spiritual fathers and mothers are, and how to walk out these relationships. Larry's writings come from both his heart and Gods heart. Healing, clarity, encouragement, revelation, and guidelines for successful relationships are all found in this needed book. You will be deeply moved and greatly helped whether you are a spiritual son or daughter or a spiritual father or mother!! I will be putting this book in the hands of our Rally Call Leadership Network family of which I am honored to serve.

Bob Long
Rally Call Leadership Network
Rally Call Ministries
San Marcos, Texas

******

The Spirit of Fatherhood is on target with what Holy Spirit is releasing over his sons and daughters in this hour. A spiritual father to us and many others, Apostle Larry has modeled and pioneered this message as a living epistle. His impartation of fatherhood is evident to all. The time is now for the body of Christ to recognize the new generation of apostolic fathers and mothers. This book is basic training for those willing to release the heart of the Father. We highly recommend it for churches, small groups, and anyone seeking to walk in greater revelation of the Father's heart.

Pastors Jack and Marti Landis
City Harvest Ministries, Liberty, Ohio

******

Larry does an excellent job of showing the divine Father-Son relationship and the human father-son relationship (which also includes daughters, of course). For many years we have admiringly observed him being a loving father to his sons and daughters-in-law as well as numerous sons/daughters in the Lord. This book is saturated with Larry's father's heart. Through that heart so many more people will now be able to see those divine and human relationships in healthy context and embrace the Fatherhood of God Almighty and they will be able to grasp how it is possible to have such a relationship with the mighty, feeling, loving Father-God. Also, he has shown that essential ensuing step where sons/daughters not only realize their sonship but they engage in their Kingdom purpose with the rights and authority of sons. Further, there is no doubt every reader will want to embrace the decrees Larry's father-heart makes over sons/daughters in *The Spirit of Fatherhood*. I have no doubt that churches and Bible study groups will be using this book as a study/discussion guide and see lives changed as did numerous others with his book The Orphan Heart.

Marty Gabler
SEEC Ministries International
Coldspring, Texas

******

Larry Burden's new book, *The Spirit of Fatherhood*, is a treasure for those who are engaged in mentoring others in order to reproduce spiritual fathers for the Kingdom of God. The Christian Church worldwide lacks these types of fathers that can give a clear representation of Jesus' character to a dying world. Having known Larry for a period of 30 years, I can tell you that he exemplifies a mature spiritual father to those who will accept his fatherhood. The book lays out in logical fashion a progression of building spiritual father/son relationships starting with the best example we can find: the relationship between our heavenly Father and his Son, Jesus Christ. The book gives an excellent picture of the characteristics of our heavenly Father and his eternal love for his future children through his love for his only begotten son, Jesus Christ.

Jack D. Tuls, DMin.
Remote Area Ministry
Lancaster, CA

******

There has never been a time in American history when the presence of fathers, both natural and spiritual, has been so critically needed, yet so painfully absent. That absence has left hearts, homes, and a nation in crisis. Larry Burden's book, *The Spirit of Fatherhood*, not only speaks powerfully to the divine call for fathers to rise in the Spirit of God's fathering heart for the healing of families and a nation, but it also is a training manual for knowing the heart of *Abba* Father and maturing as His son or daughter. Filled with rich insights, revelation, and thought-provoking questions, this book will both change the way you see God and His Fathering care in your life and mature you to be a spiritual father or mother to others in a time when it is so critically needed. This book is timely and a must read!

J. Nicole Williamson
President - King's Lantern Ministries
Plano, Texas

******

The revelation the Father has given to Apostle Larry will shift and change your life, for he takes us into the depth of God's heart for relationship with His Body. It moves us from seeing God sitting on His throne to seeing and experiencing God in our lives personally.

God the Father desires to walk and talk with us and to lead and guide us, so much so, that we become His eyes, His voice, and His love manifested in the earth

This book will realign your life and cause you to walk in a deeper awareness of Christ in you.

Tricia Miller
Miller International Inc.
Tyler, Texas

******

Many people describe those alive today as a "fatherless generation." Larry Burden's book, *The Spirit of Fatherhood*, deals with this current crisis. He compels readers to shift from a slave mentality to a covenant son relationship with Father God. Sons receive an inheritance. Slaves do not! Read Larry's book and receive an impartation from the Father's heart. There is an inheritance reserved for sons of God in the Kingdom. That includes you!

Barbara Wentroble
President: International Breakthrough Ministries, Inc.
Author: *Walking in Your Life's Purpose; You are Anointed with Fire; Releasing the Voice of the Ekklesia*
Website: www.barbarawentroble.com
Email: info@barbarawentroble.com

*****

I consider it such a great honor to write this endorsement for Apostle Larry Burden.

This book is a beautifully comprehensive work on the various aspects of Kingdom fathering written by a true father of the faith. It is easy to understand and important for current times. As God awakens the earth, people are going to be running to the church to be fathered. This book is a tool to help the church get ready!

Melissa Gabler
SEEC Ministries International
Coldspring, Texas

Table of Contents

Foreword 1

Introduction 5

1. Knowing the Father 9

2. The Mission of Jesus 21

3. The Father-Son Relationship 29

4. The Qualities of Mature Sons 37

5. Understanding Spiritual Fatherhood 49

6. The Spirit of Fatherhood 61

7. A New Generation of Apostolic Fathers and Mothers 75

Biography 85

Dedication

To Dr. Kenneth and Dorothy Speak
To Dr. Jack and Grace Tuls
To Mel and Barbara Kunau
To Jim and Jean Hodges

This book has been inspired through four father and mother relationships that have not only impacted my life and family but also countless lives and families of many sons and daughters over the past four decades. We have been so very blessed to receive your love, counsel, encouragement, direction, and correction throughout the duration of our years of ministry, training, and individual maturation. To say that we love you deeply would be the understatement of a lifetime. We honor The Father in honoring you. With all our love, respect, and deepest appreciation, thank you for never giving up on us. Thank you for giving selflessly of yourselves to us through your love, training, encouragement, correction, and being there in our most trying days. May you receive the highest blessings from The Father for your labors of love and may your impartations into our lives continue through us, one and all, and into the generations to come.

Acknowledgements

My sincere thanks to Sally May for sharing her insight and encouragement to personally motivate me to begin and complete this book. I so appreciate your expertise to edit the initial manuscript, to make recommendations that improved the quality of the message of fatherhood, and for formatting the final version of this book for publication. Thank you too for sharing your expertise of publishing options.

I further express my deep appreciation to Dr. Dana Sleger for her meticulous labors in the final editing of the manuscript and wise counsel in presenting the content. It was indeed an honor to have your support and counsel in this important message of the Spirit of Fatherhood.

My heartfelt gratitude to Melissa Gabler for reviewing the initial manuscript and providing encouragement to complete this project. Thank you for your prophetic insight and support throughout the process. You are indeed a precious gift and woman of honor.

Finally, my gratitude to artist Steve Uriegas for the creative inspiration that led to the artwork for the book cover. I not only appreciate your gift but also your heart to freely share your excellent works of art with so many. I highly recommend you to those who appreciate and seek creative artists, and I am honored to share your website at steveuriegas.com.

Foreword

by Jim Hodges

Larry Burden is an authentic spiritual father and a true spiritual son. He and I have walked together for 22 years in life and Kingdom ministry. He and his wonderful family are very dear to Jean and me.

Therefore, I am honored to write the Foreword to this powerful and insightful book! His first book, *The Orphan Heart*, is a best-seller, and I predict this volume will have a larger readership within the Body of Christ.

Larry's journey in God, the Father, and his journey with spiritual parents, are unveiled in these pages. Larry is not talking theory in this very readable presentation; he is talking life and reality in the Kingdom of God!

With biblical accuracy and theological acumen, the author presents a profound study of the fatherhood of God, the fatherhood of Jesus, and spiritual fatherhood, all of which we read about in both the Old Covenant and New Covenant. These three dimensions of authentic fatherhood and parenthood will deliver, restore, and guide all who embrace them! No one will read this book and remain the same. The questions that follow each chapter are very helpful in defining our need for true fatherhood and for guiding us forward in our journey of faith. The truths in this volume will impart spiritual understanding and will release practical application of transformative truth!

Larry's analysis of contemporary life and culture prophetically point to the truths found in Malachi 4:5-6. We see in the following verses the strategies for reversing the curse of fatherlessness and the releasing the blessing of fatherhood. Let's take a look at the passage: "Remember the law of Moses My servant, even the statutes and ordinances which I commanded him in Horeb for all Israel. Behold I am going to send you Elijah the prophet before the coming of the great and terrible day of the Lord. He will restore the hearts of the fathers to their children and the hearts of the children to their fathers, so that I will not come and smite the land with a curse". Notice these truths: Elijah modeled spiritual fatherhood to Elisha who was faithful to him and thus rewarded by a 'double portion' of Elijah's anointing. (2) Through the father-son relationship, God set the pattern for reconnecting the generations and removing the curse on the nation of Israel. (3) The curse of fatherlessness in a nation can be reversed by the restoration of true fatherhood and parenthood. (4) The spirit of Elijah was upon John the Baptizer who was sent by God to introduce the ministry of the Lord Jesus. Jesus modeled true sonship by always obeying God the Father, and He modeled true fatherhood by discipling His followers in the ways of the Father.

Let me encourage you to read, study, and pray with Apostle Larry through this book. It will change you in ways that will amaze you.

Jim Hodges
Founder and President
Federation of Ministers and Churches International

Introduction

A Fox News headline on a video from June 17, 2022, stated, "Lack of Father Figure Leading to Poor Proficiency in Education" (Fox News, June 17, 2022). As Father's Day approached, the article further explained, Data from the United States Census Bureau shows that nearly 18.5 million children grow up without their fathers, which has in return led to the United States owning the title of the world's leader in fatherlessness. What a disturbing and disgraceful statistic for any nation to own. America is indeed in crisis.

Fatherhood is critical to the healthy growth and development of our children. Children with engaged fathers in the household have a healthier life, exhibit greater academic performance, are more emotionally and socially secure, and achieve a more prosperous future when compared to those without fathers in the home. Statistics vary, but at the time of this writing, the Fox News video report continued to report that approximately 80% of single parent homes are being led by single mothers.

The report further stated that higher incidences of behavior disorders, drug and alcohol addiction, adolescent crime and gang violence are all attributed primarily to children being reared in fatherless homes. This not only has a negative effect upon the children, but also the communities where these children live. Further, as these children grow into adulthood, they have little natural or emotional wherewithal to engage productively in the culture. Most will become poverty stricken and an added burden to society. This is not fair to our children or the culture.

While governments have considered legislation to provide incentives for two-parent homes, provide support for at-risk youth, and develop programs to help struggling fathers, no legislation can reach the heart of this matter. With all due respect, until one has a genuine encounter with the fatherhood of God and meaningful relationships with natural and spiritual fathers to guide and model, I see no improvement ahead in these discouraging statistics.

We are a fatherless generation in desperate need of healthy fatherhood and motherhood. Our children need the understanding of their identity as sons or daughters. Our children need stability of soul and confidence in a hopeful future - attributes that can only be instilled through mature fathers and mothers who are responsible for teaching and training them. The current cultural climate of our nation does not promote a healthy family environment for our children to flourish. It then falls upon us, the Church, the body of Christ, the fathers and mothers of the faith, to tackle the enormous task of reshaping the lives of the generations to become healthy, productive sons and daughters.

The Spirit of Fatherhood is written to address the critical hour in which we are living, to describe the fatherhood of God, to discuss the needs and virtues of true father and motherhood, and to reshape the generations of children by actively engaging their lives as fathers and mothers of the faith. Not only is America counting on us; heaven is counting on us as well. We were born for such a time as this, and it is time for us to arise and take our place of influence in the future of our nations, children, our spiritual offspring, and heritage.

1
Knowing the Father

In Genesis 1:1, the Bible states, *In the beginning God.* The Hebrew word here for God is *Elohim*, the title that best characterizes His plural majesty. He is like a pristine diamond of limitless facets. When gazing upon Him, it appears that you have a grasp of His brilliance only for Him to turn ever so slightly to reveal another facet of His deity yet unseen and unknown. He is the sovereign God of heaven and earth. He is the Holy God of justice. He is the relational God of Abraham, Isaac, and Jacob. He is the God who can be trusted. He is the God of mercy and kindness. He is the God of righteousness and strength. He is as near as your breath and next heartbeat. He is this and limitless more. He is Eternal God.

The root of *Elohim* is *El*, the term used in ancient times to describe His deity. It was also used in Old Testament times to describe His revealed power. He is the God who delivered Israel from Egypt. He is the God who provided supernatural provision. He is the God who fights our battles and protects us. *El* is used in the names that describe God. *El Elyon* is God Most High. *El Shaddai* is God Almighty. *El Olam* is Everlasting God. *El Roi* is the God who sees me. Of course, there are more names of God that describe His nature and character, His heart and soul, and more.

God also is described in the Old Testament as *Ab*, meaning Father. In the Bible, we see God not only as all-powerful, but also as an all-loving Father. Moses described this in Deuteronomy 32:6 where he states, *Do you thus repay the Lord, O foolish people and unwise? Is not He your FATHER [Ab] that has brought you? Has He not made you, and established you?* Moses describes Ab as the Father who birthed and protected the Israelites and, as such, should be honored as their Father.

In Psalm 68, David writes about the true God. In verse 1 he begins by saying, Let God (*Elohim*) arise, let His enemies be scattered: let them also that hate Him flee before Him. He speaks of God as the warrior God who subdues all who war against Him. Then in verse 5, David pens, *A Father (Ab) of the fatherless, and a judge of the widows, is God (Elohim) in His holy habitation.* The word *judge* is translated "advocate." An advocate is one who stands alongside another and supports them. The *holy habitation* speaks of His innermost being. It reveals the nature and character of His heart. He is a loving, caring Creator God who intensely loves and cares for His creation. We, as man represent His greatest creative work and therefore receive

His greatest love and full support in this life as His offspring. He fights for us.

The prophet Malachi poses a question in Malachi 2:10, *Have we not all one Father (Ab)? Has not one God (El) created us?* Clearly the all-powerful *El*, who created the heavens and the earth and all who dwell therein, upholds us with His mighty strength and advocates for us throughout our lives as the loving, caring Father *(Ab)* that He is. David and Solomon were two son-kings that God fathered in the Old Testament. Of Solomon, God said, *I will be his Father (Ab), and he shall be my son. If he commits iniquity, I will chasten him with the rod of men, and with the stripes of the children of men; but my mercy shall not depart away from him as I took it from Saul, whom I put away before you* (2 Samuel 7:14).

The Father is revealed to us through His Son. In John 14:6-9 (NLT) the Bible records, Jesus told him (Thomas), *I am the way, the truth, and the life. No one can come to the Father except through me ... Philip said, Lord, show us the Father, and we will be satisfied. Jesus replied, have I been with you all this time, Philip, and yet you still don't know who I am? Anyone who has seen ME has seen THE FATHER!*

The way we embrace the fatherhood of God is by receiving and embracing His Son. Jesus knew Father as *Abba*, and so are we to know Him as *Abba*. Jesus cried out to Father in Gethsemane before enduring the cross, saying, *Abba Father, all things are possible for you. Take away this cup from me. Yet I want your will, not mine* (Mark 14:36 TLB).

Abba is an Aramaic word for *Father*, much like our words, *Daddy*, or *Papa*. *Abba* is an expression of childlike trust. When addressing Father, it is a word that speaks of total confidence and security in a father who will always and forever have our best interests in his heart. And Jesus is the entrance for all mankind to enter into a union of oneness of heart with *Abba*. He is the ONLY entrance or door to have a living, productive relationship with *Abba*.

Love and the Father's Heart

Love is the key that unlocks the door to the Father's heart! Several favorite Bible verses that support this include the following:

John 3:16-17 (TPT), *For this is how much God loved the world – He gave His one and only Son as a gift. So now everyone who believes in Him will never perish but experience everlasting life. God did not send his Son into the world to judge and condemn the world, but to be its Savior and rescue us.*

1 John 3:1-3 (TPT), *Look with wonder at the depth of the Father's marvelous love that he has lavished on us! He has called us and made us his very own beloved children. The reason the world doesn't recognize who we are is that they didn't recognize him. Beloved, we are God's children right now; however, it is not yet apparent what we will become. But we know that when it is finally made visible, we will be just like him, for we will see him as he truly is. And all who focus their hope on him will always be purifying themselves, just as Jesus is pure.*

1 John 4:16 (TPT), *We have come into an intimate experience with God's love, and we trust in the love he has for us.*

> Love is the key that unlocks the door to the Father's heart!

Through love, the Father revealed himself to us through Jesus. Jesus said, *I have manifested your name to the men you have given me out of the world. They were yours, you gave them to me, and they have kept your word ... and I have declared to them your name and will declare it, that the love with which you loved me may be in them, and I in them* (John 17:6, 26 NKJV). Jesus was saying that he had revealed the genuine heart and Spirit of God's fatherhood to his disciples. Jesus modeled this and imparted it by Holy Spirit.

So, how did Jesus reveal the Father to the disciples and ultimately to us who have received his salvation and now have true, genuine relationship with the Father, *Abba*?

First, by his teaching. Jesus seized every opportunity to share the message of the Father's heart toward mankind. In the Sermon on the Mount in Matthew 5, he shared that the poor in spirit will be offered the Father's kingdom. Those who mourn will be comforted by the Father. The meek will inherit Father's earth. Father will fill those who seek His righteousness. The merciful will obtain Father's mercy. The pure in heart will see Father. Peacemakers will be called Father's children, and the persecuted will receive Father's great reward. In this passage alone, Father's love and desire to bless His sons and daughters and release His love upon them is clearly revealed.

In Luke 15:11-24, Jesus reveals the restorative heart of the Father through the story of the Prodigal Son. The wayward lad demanded his rights of inheritance, left his father's house, and set out into the world to pursue his own way in life. He squandered his inheritance in sinful living and ended up tending a farmer's pigs, where he was so hungry that the pig's food began to look good to him. He came to his senses, recalled that his father's servants had a better life than his, and in humility, he determined to return to his father where he planned to repent, forfeit his position of a son, and seek employment as one of the father's hired servants.

While approaching his father's house, this son did not notice his father was peering down the road, no doubt hoping for his son to return. When he saw his son from afar, the father raced to meet him, swept him into his arms, hugged and kissed him *over and over with tender love* (Luke 15:20). The son repented and stated he no longer deserved to be his father's son, but as he was speaking, the father interrupted him. The father immediately called for his best robe to place on his son's shoulders thereby restoring the father covering over his son. He called for a ring to be placed upon his finger as a seal of authority of sonship and authority to transact the father's business. He brought out the best shoes he could find to place upon his son's feet (only slaves walked barefoot). He finally ordered a great feast to celebrate the new life for his son. The father stated, *For this beloved son of mine was once dead, but now he's alive again. Once he was lost, but now he is found. And everyone celebrated with overflowing joy.* (Luke 15:24 TPT).

The second way Jesus revealed the heart of the Father to humanity was though his own personal life. He reflected the Father's love in the manner in which He interacted with humanity. One of the best examples of this is his encounter with the woman at the well (John 4:1-42). Jesus had been drawing large crowds in Jerusalem as he taught and healed many when he abruptly departed with his disciples to journey to Samaria. This was alarming to his disciples since Samaria was not a destination spot for any self-respecting Jew to travel. Jews had little to do with Samaritans and less with the women of Samaria.

As Jesus approached the Samaritan village of Sychar, he became thirsty and stopped at Jacob's well. He sat on the edge of the well and sent the disciples into the village to purchase food. While sitting alone atop the well, a Samaritan woman approached to fill her waterpots. Jesus spoke to her saying, *Give me a drink of water.* Stunned that this Jewish man would speak to her, the woman inquired why he would dare ask her for a drink. This was the beginning of the longest recorded conversation that Jesus would have with a single individual in all the gospels. He ultimately revealed to her, the least likely person ever, that He was Messiah. Jesus chose the least of the least in the eyes of the culture, a Samaritan, and a scorned woman at that, to be the first to hear the good news of the love of

Father that His Son, Jesus was the chosen Messiah to remove forever the sin of Adam from all mankind.

When the woman heard Jesus declare his identity, she ran to her village and spread the news about the man who knew all about her and loved her in spite of her history. The entire village rushed out to see Jesus, and He spent two days with them before moving on to Galilee. He demonstrated the Father's love to this group whom no respectable Jew would dare come near. What kind of love is this?

This Samaritan woman actually is known by name. Through hagiography—the passing down of stories orally from generation to generation—the Eastern Orthodox Church revealed her name and canonized her as a saint. Her name was Photini, meaning "Enlightened One." History records that she was baptized by the disciples and became known as the Mother of Evangelists. She was known as a bold follower of Jesus. Photini witnessed to multitudes throughout her lifetime and brought many to salvation, not only in Samaria but also throughout the surrounding regions. She was regarded an equal to the apostles by the church.

In Carthage, Photini received a vision from the Lord to travel to Rome and confront Emperor Nero. She made the journey with her family and those who followed her; and after confronting Emperor Nero as instructed by the Lord, she, and everyone with her were tortured and eventually killed. After being tortured and imprisoned,

Photini was ultimately thrown into a dry well where it is recorded that she sang and prayed aloud day and night until her death two weeks later. The natural well was dry, but the well of her heart remained full of living water. Only the love for the Father as revealed by the love of the Son could have sustained this precious woman and all of us who know this great love.

So many more teaching and life moments demonstrated by Jesus are found throughout the gospels, and volumes are written on each one. The summation of them all is that the Father was reflected in his life. Jesus said, *He who has seen me has seen the Father* (John 14:9 NASB). He also said, *Believe me that I am in the Father and the Father is in me ... the words that I speak unto you I speak not of myself, but the Father who sent me.* (John 14:10). When praying prior to his crucifixion, Jesus said to the Father, *I have manifested your name unto the men that you gave me out of the world; thine they were, and you gave them to me; and they have kept your word* (John 17:6).

This life of the Father has also been imparted to us who are seekers of the Father's heart. Jesus prayed, *Neither do I pray for these alone, but for them also which SHALL BELIEVE ON ME through their word; that they may be one as you, Father, are in me, and I in you, that they may also be one in us; that the world may believe that you have sent me. And the glory which you gave me, I have given them, that they may be one, even as we are one* (John 17:20-22).

We as the sons and daughters of the Father through the Son Jesus, our Savior and Elder Brother, have been given the greatest gift of all mankind—oneness with the Father.

Chapter 1: Knowing the Father Review

In Chapter 1, we explored the character and nature of our Heavenly Father.

He is:

- Holy God of Justice
- Sovereign
- Relational
- Trustworthy
- Righteous and Strong
- Merciful and Kind
- Eternal
- Limitless
- Provider
- Protector
- *Abba* (Pappa/Daddy)

Questions:

1. Describe the relationship between you and your earthly father.
2. How does your relationship with your earthly father influence your perspective of Heavenly Father?
3. When you think of Heavenly Father, which characteristics immediately come to mind?
4. Describe the characteristics of Heavenly Father that you have personally experienced.
5. Name characteristics of Heavenly Father that you struggle with embracing or accepting. Why?

2
The Mission of Jesus

John 1:1 reveals that Jesus was the Word who was present in the beginning (Genesis 1:1) with God (*Elohim*). *All things came into being through Him, and apart from Him nothing came into being that has come into being. In Him was life, and the life was the light of men* (John 1:3-4 NASB). So, the Father and the Son were united together before the very beginning of creation. The word *beginning* is the Greek word *arche*, which means "to be first." Jesus and *Elohim* were together at the first of all things in heaven and earth before creation ever existed. In the origin of God's creation, the Father and Son were in harmony or oneness.

The word *beginning* also speaks of "rule and ruler or leader." More importantly, the word beginning speaks to a cause. The term "word" is *logos*, which means "the expressions of thought." These thoughts are the thoughts of God Himself. The expressions of the thoughts of Father are recorded throughout the 66 books of the Bible. So, *logos* can be a word as the expression of the thoughts of Father, a discourse, an orderly linking and knitting together in connected arrangements of words of the inward thoughts and feelings of the mind of Father Himself. In order for us to understand the heart of these discourses, we must make room in our hearts to receive that word of His life. This could only be accomplished through Jesus, THE WORD.

Jesus is the *Son of God* and *Personal Word* that opens the hearts of men to receive the heartfelt truths of the Father. Jesus is called *The Beginning* because He is the effective cause of creation. He is the Head because He is before all things and all things were created by Him and FOR Him. The cause of Jesus in the earth is to perpetuate the Father-Son relationship in the earth realm as the mirror image of The Father-Son relationship in the heaven realm. Jesus was and remains today the Father's cause. From the very beginning of all things as we know it, Father determined that the relationship with Himself and Jesus would be perpetuated throughout all the generations of mankind.

We are fearfully, wonderfully, and uniquely made in the same image and likeness of the Father and Son. Paul declared, *The first man Adam became a living soul. The last Adam became the life-giving Spirit* (1 Corinthians 15:45). So then, we are born into the earth as a living soul and born again into the eternal realm as His life-giving Spirit. This is the Spirit of the Father in operation through all of His sons and daughters. The Father-Son relationship which was in place before time began was key in creation and Father's original intent for all mankind.

John declared that the light of the Father was in the Son (John 1: 4-5). This life was the light of His Spirit that illuminates the inner man. Proverbs 20:27 declares, *The spirit of a man is the candle of the Lord, searching all the inward parts of the belly.* Jesus carried the life of the Father in His spirit. His spirit was illuminated like a candle illuminates a dark space. Our spirit becomes illuminated by the Holy Spirit when we receive Jesus as our Lord and Savior. In the very core of our being there comes the inner witness in our hearts that we are indeed the sons and daughters of the Living God.

This light in the core of our being is God in Spirit. This life can never be put out. This fire can never be extinguished. It is eternal and thereby shines forevermore! No darkness can choke it out. No pressures can put out the flame—trials and testing only fan the flames hotter and brighter. When the Holy Spirit shines into our hearts, we become instantly alive to the knowledge of the Father. We know that The Father has become our Father.

Whether anyone ever sees or acknowledges the light of Father inside us, the light of Holy Spirit is there, residing in our being. The stars in the sky shine continually whether anyone gazes upon them or not. The sun and moon shine whether we ever look at them or not. We do, however, see the light shining around us without having to look directly at it.

The Son Jesus fulfilled the Father's cause in the earth for all of us throughout all generations by illuminating every heart with the opportunity to become one with the Father. Only a darkened soul, filled with depravity, can be blinded to the light of the Father. A soul held captive by the orphan spirit is unable to seize the truth and life and light of this cause of fatherhood both exhibited by and extended to ALL through Jesus.

Jesus remains the true *Light of the world* (John 8:12) who illuminates every soul of man to the understanding of the reconciliation between Father and man. His light is meant to cause all men to see the Father and bring reconciliation between the two. The Father seeks to restore all men to His original design of union with His sons and daughters. When Jesus entered the earth in the flesh, the Bible says that many did not know Him (John 1:10). He came to unite His own with the Father, but they did not receive Him. But others did recognize and receive Him, and those who did were given the authority of the Father to become His sons and daughters with full rights and privileges.

The primary purpose of salvation was never intended for us to build our personal kingdoms or to simply enjoy the miracles, signs and wonders, and benefits of our father-son relationship with *Abba*. The primary cause was to break the curse of fatherlessness described by the prophet Malachi (Malachi 4:6) and to destroy the orphan spirit by restoring the genuine father-son relationships in the earth.

As sons and daughters, we are the reborn of God (John 1:13). We have been regenerated as the procreation of the Father. This came not by human means or our own design nor by any human operation. It was and continues to be the ultimate will of the Father through His Son. He was made flesh and lived among man on earth, and John and others *beheld His glory, the glory of the only begotten of the Father, full of grace and truth* (John 1:14). The original language of the Bible says that Jesus *pitched His tent* among us to tabernacle with us as the One and Only begotten Son of Father God.

Jesus is the only son ever to be eternal in origin and become born of flesh. Through Him, we as the flesh born sons of origin became eternal sons through eternal rebirth. He was born into the earth by the Father, He came to restore us to the Father, and to those who receive Him as Father become eternal sons with Jesus.

John saw this clearly, and he recorded what he saw in 1 John 1:1-4:

That which was from the beginning, which we have heard, which we have seen with our eyes, which we have looked upon, and our hands have handled, of the Word of Life. For the life was manifested and we have seen it, and bear witness, and show to you that eternal life, which was with the Father and was manifested to us. That which we have seen and heard, we declare to you so that you also may have fellowship with us, and our fellowship is with the Father and with His Son Jesus Christ.

The invitation never ceases, and the heart of the Father never grows cold. He continues as long as the earth exists to reach out to His beloved creation to reverse the curse of Adam in our lives and restore us to oneness with His heart through the Son Jesus, and that we might govern His earth as He originally intended.

Chapter 2: The Mission of Jesus Review

In Chapter 2, we discover the mission of Jesus on earth was to restore our relationship with our Heavenly Father.

Questions:

1. How was the original design for your relationship with Heavenly Father aborted?
2. How does the feeling of being fatherless impact someone?
3. How is the original design for your relationship with our Heavenly Father restored?
4. Describe your current relationship with the Heavenly Father.
5. Have you had difficulty accepting that you are no longer fatherless? Why?

3

The Father-Son Relationship

In Exodus 3, Moses is in Midian where he is on the run from his father, Pharaoh. He had killed an Egyptian who was beating a Hebrew slave and now his Pharaoh father was seeking him out for execution. In Midian, Moses married the daughter of a priest, and her name was Zipporah. For 40 years, Moses lived in Midian and tended sheep. Following Pharaoh's death in Egypt, God appeared to Moses in a burning bush, and this glory manifestation of the Father commanded Moses' recognition and response.

Moses approached the bush to see what this amazing display was all about. As he did, God spoke, *I am the God (Elohim) of your father, the God of Abraham, the God of Isaac, and the God of Jacob, and Moses hid his face; for he was afraid to look upon God* (Exodus 3:6 NASB). Father identified Himself as the God of Moses' father, which signifies not only his natural father Aram, the son of Levi, but also his adopted father, Pharaoh.

God then delivered a message and an assignment to Moses in verses 7-10. He said, *I have surely seen the affliction of my people who are in Egypt and have given heed to their cry because of their taskmasters, for I am aware of their sufferings. So I have come down to deliver them from the power of the Egyptians, and to bring them up from that land to a good and spacious land, to a land flowing with milk and honey, to the place of the Canaanite and the Hittite, and the Amorite and the Perizzite and the Hivite and the Jebusite* (NASB). God then instructed Moses that HE was going to deliver Israel through Moses.

Why did God choose Moses? He was chosen because he was a SON—a son of a covenant father through the tribe of Levi and an adopted son of Pharaoh of Egypt. He was also carried in the heart of Father God as a son by divine appointment. In Exodus 7:1 (AMP), the scripture says, *The Lord said to Moses, Behold, I have made you as God to Pharaoh [to declare my will and purpose to him]; and Aaron your brother shall be your prophet.* This was one of the first Apostle-Prophet teams in the Bible. The words, *as God to Pharaoh* means "Like Me to Pharaoh." God was telling Moses that he was a son, not only to his earthly father Aram, and to his adopted father Pharaoh, but more importantly a son of the Living Covenant God. Inheritance is reserved for covenant sons, not slaves.

Moses obeys the Lord, delivers Israel from Egypt as instructed, and ultimately inherits a nation of orphans.

They are so rebellious, demanding, and entitlement-minded that even God wanted to get rid of the entire lot and start over building a nation with Moses alone. They complained so much that Moses also wanted God to just kill them and end his suffering. Yet, when God disclosed to Moses that he was going to destroy them, Moses stepped up as a father to implore God to repent of this thought, not because he wanted the Israelites to be spared, but because he did not want the nations to develop the wrong view of God's Fatherhood. The heart of the Father was truly entrenched into Moses.

In Numbers 3, the nation finally arrives at the gateway to the Promised Land. Twelve spies are sent out to recon the territory. Ten of the spies return with a negative report while two return with a report of faith. In spite of all that the Father had done to prove His Fatherhood to this nation, the orphan spirit was too entrenched in their mindsets for them to see through to victory and blessing. Only Joshua and Caleb had a different spirit – the spirit of sonship. When it finally came time for a new generation to cross over the Jordan 40 years later and to take possession of the promised inheritance of God, it was a son, Joshua, who led them forward to make that promise a reality.

The Lord told Moses before the crossing of the Jordan to, *Take Joshua, the son of Nun, a man in whom is the Spirit, and lay your hand upon him; and set him before Eleazar the priest, and before all the congregation, and give him a charge in their sight. And you shall put some of your honor upon him, that all the congregation of the children of Israel may be obedient* (Numbers 27: 18-20). The word *Spirit* (*ruach*) is translated "wind, breath, mind." Joshua carried the *wind* of the Father, the *breath* of the Father's life, and the *mindset* of a son. The *honor* imparted to Joshua through the laying on of Moses' hand was the glory of the Fatherhood of God.

Joshua as a son received an impartation from his Heavenly Father through the impartation that the Heavenly Father had given his spiritual father Moses. Scripture would later reveal that this impartation was the Spirit of Wisdom. Father God released from His glory an impartation into Moses, and Moses released that impartation from Father God into Joshua as a Spiritual Father to a Spiritual Son. Joshua had to receive this as a son because only sons can receive from a father, slaves do not know how.

Inheritance is reserved for covenant sons, not slaves. Joshua's assignment was not only to take possession of Canaan. He was also to perpetuate the generations of fathers and sons. Ultimately, Jesus Himself was required for the Father to come into earth and, once and for all time, establish the eternal order of Fatherhood and sonship.

We are no doubt living in the time of inheritance. We have been destined to take dominion over the earth as sons of the Father. So, why have we not received this already? That question takes me back to the first church I was ever called to pastor. The congregation was made up of precious saints that loved God with all their hearts. However, I always wondered why there were no signs, wonders, and miracles in that little church. When I asked the Lord why these promises were not manifesting, he answered me, *Because you do not know yet how to appropriate them.* Unknowingly at the time, the Father was letting me know that I had an orphan heart and mindset. Sons know how to appropriate the miracles of Father. Sons receive the inheritance of the supernatural by trusting and walking in oneness with the Father. Faith for miracles come by hearing the Word of the Father as a son.

True fathers are those who are actively engaged in the lives of their sons and daughters. They assist their offspring in learning the ways of the Spirit. They impart knowledge and wisdom into their children and grandchildren and assist them in deciding their future. Genuine father hearts always have your best interests in their hearts.

True fathers can be trusted. Trust is a huge issue in father-son relationships. You cannot trust everyone in life, but whenever God determines to bless you, he will oftentimes place a father or mother gift close to you with an instruction and an encouragement for you and your future. One will never advance in this life without trusting someone; this is a principle of life. What has been given to you by the Father is almost always to be a blessing for someone else. Maybe it is to improve another person's life in some way. Maybe it is to simply be a blessing to another. Maybe it is to speak a word that will develop another, or maybe it is to bring a course correction into someone's life. Ultimately, fathers and mothers are used to help shape and mold the lives of their spiritual children to enlarge the Father's kingdom agenda in the earth.

One's ability to trust the father that God has given you can be the difference between remarkable success or miserable failure. I endeavor to surround myself with trusted fathers and mothers of the faith whom I can trust. I also do the same with father and mother gifts that are spiritually stronger and wiser than I am. I need their wisdom and instruction to keep me advancing in the right direction. Not every word is for me and not everyone around me has a place to speak into my life. However, I listen and take heart to the words from those with whom I am aligned and those who have been divinely placed around me as influencers from the Father. I highly recommend the same for you.

Chapter 3: The Father-Son Relationship Review

In Chapter 3, we reviewed the life of Moses and how God chose Moses to be the Father of Israel. God is looking for men and women to be spiritual fathers and mothers to the next generation.

Questions:

1. Describe the relationship between a spiritual father/mother and their son/daughter.
2. Name characteristics of a spiritual parent. Which ones are most important to you? Why?
3. As a spiritual child, what are your expectations of your spiritual parent?
4. If you have never had a spiritual father or mother, have you prayed and asked God to manifest that individual in your life?
5. Do you find it is difficult to trust someone to speak into your life? Why?

4

The Qualities of Mature Sons

In Acts 3, the Bible records a divine encounter between Apostle Peter and a lame man as Peter and John were enroute to the temple to pray. In those days, sacrifices were made at the temple at sunrise and around 3 pm each afternoon, and it was at the 3 o'clock hour that Peter and John were making their way to prayer. They made their way to the entrance of the temple known as the Beautiful Gate. In Aramaic, this was translated as "the Gate called Wonderful," and this particular gate represented Jesus as the gate into the sheepfold of the Father. The gate also reflects the gate in Ezekiel 47 that has a river flowing from the threshold through the gateway of the temple. Ezekiel's river was first measured at ankle deep, corresponding to the man with crippled ankles whom Peter would soon encounter.

As Peter and John approached the entrance to the gate, this lame man who was crippled in the ankles from birth, caught sight of them and begged for money. Clearly the heart of Father was moved with compassion for this man on this day. In Acts 3:6 (TPT), the Holy Spirit responded, and Peter stopped, fastened his eyes upon the man, and said, *I don't have money, but I'll give you this – by the power of the name of Jesus Christ of Nazareth, stand up and walk!* With his right hand, Peter pulled the man to his feet. Immediately, his feet and ankles were infused by the power of Holy Spirit, and he stood up, began to walk, and finally jumped with joy as he followed Peter and John into the temple courts.

The crowd in the temple courts heard and recognized this man whom they had known for years, and were completely astounded to see him whole. They rushed over to Peter and John who had the lame man clinging to them, and Peter seized the moment to preach the gospel of the resurrected Christ. When he finished preaching, 5,000 men repented of their sin and committed their hearts to Jesus in salvation.

In Acts 4, the priests, the captain of the temple police, and the Sadducees were furious that Peter and John were declaring the resurrection of Jesus. The Jewish authorities immediately had Peter and John arrested and thrown into jail. The next day they were brought before the temple authorities to give an account for their heresy. In verse 7, the High Priest demanded to know, *By what power and authority have you done these things?* It is in this moment that we see the qualities of a mature son who is becoming a strong father gift.

The first quality of a mature son is being continually filled with the Holy Spirit. *Peter, filled with the Holy Spirit, answered...* (Acts 4 8). In the original language this verse actually states, *having just been filled with the Holy Spirit....* On the Day of Pentecost Peter, along with the other 119 in the upper room had been baptized in the Holy Spirit and fire. But days had passed since the initial filling of the power of the Spirit. Acts 4:26 states, *And day by day, continuing with one mind in the temple, and breaking bread from house to house, they were taking their meals together with gladness of heart.* That tells me that the apostles were in daily prayer and fellowship, keeping the fire of Holy Spirit stoked and intensively hotter by the day. The fire of Holy Spirit on this day was not from the afterglow of Pentecost—it was a fresh filling of the day. Paul states in Romans 8:14 that mature sons of God are governed by the Spirit of God. The inference is that they remain filled each day with Holy Spirit fire.

Paul also says in Ephesians 5:18, *And don't get drunk with wine, which is rebellion, instead be filled with the fullness of the Holy Spirit* (TPT). He was saying that we are to be inebriated with the Holy Spirit! When Peter was asked by what power and authority that he healed the lame man, he released that recharged power of the new day and shook the religious elite's assumptive world. If we, as mature sons and daughters, are going to be used of the Father to shake up the systems of religion and the evil civil rule of nations, we must be continually filling up our spirit man with Holy Spirit fire. We must keep our spirit charged up with Holy Spirit fire to be ready when a need is demanded of us.

The second quality of a mature son is confidence that comes from spending quality time with Father. Acts 4:13 says that the Council members were astonished as they witnessed the bold courage of Peter and John, especially when they discovered that they were just ordinary men who had never had religious training. Then they began to understand the effect Jesus had on Peter and John simply because they spent time with him. Their confidence was evident to the religious leaders, and they were bold and filled with authority—attributes that come only from spending quality time with Jesus. Confidence always comes from being in the presence of the Father. Hebrews 3:6 tells us that Jesus was *faithful as a Son over his house, whose house you are, if you hold fast your confidence and the boast of your hope firm to the end.*

Confidence is being full of trust and free of doubt. It is full of assurance and the authority of Jesus. It is the normal mindset of those who spend time with Father. Mature sons are worshippers since worship is one connector of sons to the Father's heart. Worship not only catapults our faith and confidence levels, it also opens our spiritual hearts to receive from the Father. One word of the Father's faith changes everything. It catapults our confidence to stand and declare His kingdom with unwavering authority and conviction. The healed lame man who stood with Peter and John was proof of their confident faith in Father, and it silenced the accusing voices of the Council.

A third quality of mature sons is intentionality. While the religious Council could not deny this notable miracle that had just taken place at the hands of Peter, they nonetheless proceeded to threaten Peter and John to speak no more to anyone else in the name of Jesus. To threaten someone is to state one's intention to take hostile action against another as a means of intimidation. They then reconvened the Council, called Peter and John before them again, and commanded them not to speak or teach at all in the name of Jesus (Acts 4:18).

Following the threats of the Council, Peter responded, *Whether it is right in the sight of God to give heed to you rather than to God, you be the judge; for we cannot stop speaking what we have seen and heard* (Acts 4:19-20 NASB). Peter made it very clear that he and John had no intention to stop teaching and preaching about the wonderful Savior Jesus Christ to anyone who had an ear to hear. He boldly declined to stop declaring that Jesus was and is the resurrected Christ.

Following this declaration, Peter and John were released to their own assembly of believers and reported the account of their events to them, where they all *lifted up their voices to God with one accord and prayed* (Acts 4:24). When they finished praying, the place where they were assembled together began to shake. They were all filled with the Holy

Spirit and began to speak the word of God with boldness (Acts 4:31). Mature sons are intentional about salvation, baptism in the Holy Spirit, speaking in tongues, healing the sick, signs, wonders, and miracles. These manifestations pursue mature sons who will yield their spirit to the Holy Spirit with intentionality and release the authority of God.

The Father delegates His power and authority to mature sons who will boldly advance His kingdom in the earth, and it is up to the Church to be intentional about this assignment. The Apostle Paul is another example of this pursuit in the face of opposition. Before heading to Rome and certain opposition, he declared in Romans 1:15-17, *Thus, I am eager to preach the gospel to you also who are in Rome. For I am not ashamed of the gospel, for it is the power of God for salvation to everyone who believes, to the Jew first and also to the Greek. For in it the righteousness of God is revealed from faith to faith; as it is written, but the righteous man shall live by faith.* Paul, the son, was very intentional about his assignment, even to the point of declaring the gospel message in the heart of the evil civil government responsible for killing Jesus. These are the same guys that Peter ran from when Jesus was on trial and denied he ever knew Jesus.

> The Father delegates His power and authority to mature sons who will boldly advance His kingdom in the earth...

Paul did not just make the declaration, he modeled this for all of us mature sons today to follow. The message from this is that we must not be intimidated or silent about Jesus. We must not stop declaring His kingdom when others around us attempt to shut us up and shut us down.

The fourth quality of a mature son is choosing the right company to keep. When Peter and John were released from the Council, they returned to their own company (Acts 4:23). They shared their report with those of like mind, like faith, and like purpose. This company of believers executed their rights as the ecclesia and prayed in the power of agreement. In Acts 4:29-30, they agreed, *And now Lord, take note of their threats, and grant us Your boldness to speak Your word with all confidence, while You also extend Your hand to heal, and signs and wonders take place through the name of Your Holy Servant Jesus.* In the company of fellow believers, Peter and John and all who were there with them became recharged in the Holy Spirit.

It is important to note that this group was not just seeking an experience with Jesus. This was not an occasion to soak in the presence of the Lord. They were pursuing a fresh enduement of the power from on high that began on the Day of Pentecost in order to speak louder and stronger in the face of opposition. This was a war season; it was not a time to be refreshed but rather a time to be recharged for spiritual battle. Peter and John chose the right company to join forces with to take a stand, and to be a voice and a presence of God's authority and power. Mature sons know how to align with the right company for the right season.

Mature sons are the product of mature fathers. Before Peter became the bold apostle of Acts, he was a simple fisherman in the Sea of Galilee. He was colorful and very outspoken. Outwardly he projected confidence and boldness, while inwardly he was full of insecurity and fear. His time with Jesus and his encounters with the Father nurtured and developed him into this bold man who faced off the religious Council that threatened him to cease and desist from pursuing his divine destiny.

On the Mount of Transfiguration, (Matthew 17), Peter heard the voice of the Father say, *This is my beloved Son with whom I am well pleased; listen to Him.* In Caesarea Philippi, (Matthew 16) Peter received the revelation from Father that Jesus was indeed the Son of God. Jesus encouraged Peter that he had indeed heard the Father's voice in his spirit, for no man could have revealed that truth to him. Peter went through the fire of testing when he was told that in spite of his best efforts, he would ultimately deny knowing Jesus after declaring that he would die for Jesus (Luke 22).

Each of these events were divine set-ups by the Father as training and development for Peter's destiny. Yet, there was one final lesson that was the most important of all. After denying Jesus, he ran away a failure. After His resurrection, Jesus returned to Peter and restored him through love. The final test that all sons and daughters must pass is the test of love. It is up to the fathers and mothers of the faith to administer this test. Teachers and mentors can train ministers to be strong in gifts, callings, and anointings, but only true fathers and mothers can impart the love of the Father for the purpose of maturing His offspring. Holy Ghost power, confidence, intentionality, fearless boldness, and right choices are the by-products of love from the Father, which are imparted through spiritual fathers and mothers. This serves to keep sons and daughters properly grounded to focus on the matters of the kingdom that are most important.

Chapter 4: The Qualities of Mature Sons Review

In Chapter 4, the attributes of mature sons/daughters were explored. Growing in our faith become spiritually mature individuals should be the primary goal for each Christian. The qualities of a mature son or daughter are:

- Continually filled with the Holy Spirit
- Radiates confidence by spending time with the Father
- Focuses on intentionality
- Selective in council and company

Questions:

1. Review the attributes of a spiritual mature son or daughter. Which of qualities do you currently have? How did you develop them?
2. What spiritual qualities do you want to cultivate? How?
3. Which spiritual qualities are the most difficult for you? Why?
4. Name someone who could support or mentor you to develop those qualities.
5. Write a prayer asking God to lead, guide and direct you to the right person to support you in your spiritual growth. Date your prayer. Are you expecting an answer?

5
Understanding Spiritual Fatherhood

In Apostle Paul's letter to the Corinthian church, he addressed the issue of his spiritual fatherhood. In establishing behavior-order in the church, he penned these words to them, *I do not write these things to shame you, but to admonish you as my beloved children. For if you were to have countless tutors* (instructors) *in Christ, yet you would not have many fathers; for in Christ Jesus, I became your father through the gospel* (1 Corinthians 4:14-15 NASB). It was important to Paul that he remind the body—the church—that he was not simply another tutor or instructor in their lives who simply disseminated the gospel. He was addressing them as a father gift divinely assigned to by virtue of divine appointment.

The word *father* in this setting is translated "pater," and one of its meanings is "one who is advanced in the knowledge of Christ as well as a preacher/teacher of the gospel who stands in a father's place, caring for his spiritual children, such as a spiritual father." Paul distinguished himself in this letter to the spiritual sons and daughters as their spiritual father who had authority to address behaviors among them that needed correction.

Paul was a Jew who was trained under Rabbi Gamaliel. He persecuted Christians in the early church as part of his religious training and belief system. He had an encounter with Jesus on the way to Damascus to persecute more Christians, and his life changed forever. He was converted to a follower of Christ, and he became one of the greatest spiritual fathers in Bible history. His fathering spirit was activated by this encounter with the Father of all spiritual sons through the Son Jesus. In 2 Timothy 1:1, Paul addresses Timothy as, *my dearly beloved son.* In Philippians 2:19-22, Paul also states, *But I trust in the Lord Jesus to send Timothy shortly unto you, that I also may be of good comfort, when I know your state. For I have no man like-minded, who will naturally care for your state. For all seek their own, not the things which are Jesus Christ's. But you know the proof of him, that as a son with the father, he has served with me in the gospel.* In Titus 1:4, Paul address Titus as, *My own son after the common faith.*

In these two examples alone, the dynamic of spiritual fatherhood is evident and scriptural. So, why is it so important to have spiritual fathers? Also, why is it important to have spiritual mothers? The simple answer is that they are used of the Father to rear and mature the spiritual offspring. In 1991, I met with a known international minister in a Houston, Texas restaurant.

Alongside me were my wife and my spiritual mother. As I talked with this minister, I knew there was a future connection with him in ministry. That said, I was not clear exactly what that looked like.

As we sat together and discussed spiritual matters, my spiritual mom peered across the table at this minister and asked, "Have you seen Larry in the Spirit?"

The minister responded, "Yes, I have, and so have you, but he has to see it for himself."

So, as we were sitting together having a nice visit, my spiritual mother and this minister were engaged in a conversation about my future. I thought that I was part of the conversation, but then I realized I had become the object of discussion. Following that meeting, it hit me in my own spirit that the Father was connecting me to this minister for an important season in my life. This encounter impacted my life to this day, and the Father used my spiritual mother to bring it into divine order and help define and order my future.

Some years later, Father God divinely connected me to a Latter Rain prophet who took me into his heart and under his wing as a spiritual father. For years he walked with me, affirmed me, and nurtured my spiritual giftings. He trained me in Prophet ministry, and he protected me from evil agendas designed to take my life.

In the late 1990's, I ruptured the Achilles tendon in my left leg while playing basketball with some Bible school students and church staff. The injury required surgery to repair, and months of physical rehabilitation. During the first few weeks following the surgery, a six-inch blood clot formed in the deep vein of my lower left leg. It was discovered on a routine follow-up examination and required immediate hospitalization and urgent medical intervention.

As I lay in the hospital bed with anticoagulants infusing into my vein, it dawned on me that at any minute the clot could break loose, travel to my lungs, and instantly take my life. While not afraid, I was mindful of this possibility. I pondered in my heart if I was ready to see Jesus should I suddenly die. I pondered how Jesus would care for my wife and sons without me. As I pondered these and other things, the telephone beside my bed rang. I answered the call to hear the voice of my spiritual father. He told me there were evil people praying for me to die and said for me to not be concerned as this would not happen. He declared that the Father had me in His hand and was going to protect and heal me. The blood clot dissolved, the leg healed, and I remain alive today to share the testimony of the goodness of the Father and the spiritual father who interceded for me.

Some years later, I received a phone call from a former member of the ministry where I was serving at the time of this accident. The person shared about being involved as a participant in a prayer group that had been faithfully praying for God to move me out of the ministry or kill me. The person called to confess and ask my forgiveness, which I readily released. I immediately remembered the call from my spiritual father and once again thanked the Father for this precious gift in my life who stood in the gap to release protection over my life.

The most important role of spiritual fathers and mothers is impartation. There have been many father and mother gifts assigned to me throughout my life. With each one, there has been an impartation of wisdom, understanding, knowledge, counsel, and blessing. Some of this impartation was practical and some was spiritual in its substance. With each parent gift assigned to my life, these impartations helped direct and challenge me to mature and to grow from level to level and faith to faith. Even now, as I walk in my own father calling, I continually draw from the fathers of the faith in order to continue learning and growing into a greater fullness of this important gifting. The greatest work of spiritual fathering is leading the spiritual sons and daughters into intimacy with Jesus. Spiritual parenting is all about intimacy, love, and the joy of guiding the sons and daughters into that deeper relationship with The Father.

Impartation comes from spending time with those appointed to you as spiritual parents. These appointments are not always the ones that you might desire, but they are the ones divinely assigned to you for whatever season of time The Father determines to be necessary. Quality time is essential for the process of growth. Such devotion can only be accomplished through love and the heart for the family – never as a duty or obligation.

Jesus is the greatest model for us to follow when it comes to spiritual fathering. He was nurtured, protected, and trained by the best – the Father Himself. When Jesus called the 12, He simply said, *Follow me*. These men left their lives as they knew at that time and responded to the call. These 12 sons had direct access to Jesus. He had their hearts, and they had His. They were not trophies, but family. They did not have to get through locked doors, busy schedules, secretaries, and protocols to access Jesus. They were family.

> **The greatest work of spiritual fathering is leading the spiritual sons and daughters into intimacy with Jesus.**

Jesus imparted life into these 12 sons. He trained them in the ways of the Father. He encouraged them when they were in the learning and maturing process. He believed in them when no one else did. He transformed them into the fathers of the faith whose books we read today in the Bible. We are encouraged and trained by them now as sons and daughters. Jesus did not choose the elite class of the Jews. He chose the common man to train and equip for the Father's business. He took the untrained and developed them into the greatest ministry and father gifts the world has ever known. Jesus was more interested in building them than He was His own life.

Jesus continually directed the 12 to the Father more so than to Himself. His greatest joy was to see this 12 grow in their knowledge of God and mature into their life callings to establish the kingdom of His Father in the earth. He released them into ministry even when they were not fully mature. Judas was in charge of the treasury, and Peter had a huge mouth and an even greater ego. Jesus knew the 12 better than they knew themselves; however, he also knew their hearts and knew that each would fulfill their divine destinies, even Judas.

Jesus knew that 11 of the original 12 would remain faithful to the Father's business. He knew they would grow in maturity and fulfill their destinies in God. He treated them in their training years as though they were more mature than they really were. He had the utmost respect and trust in these father gifts; and he nurtured, protected, and spiritually reared them to step into their calling and destiny. These men became the greatest spiritual fathers in history.

Spiritual fathers do not seek accolades, entitlements, or positions of power. They are not after money or notoriety. They are not seekers of influence or entitlement. They simply share their hearts with the sons and daughters and point them always to true north, the heart of the Father. They live by the code of John the Baptist, *He must increase, but I must decrease* (John 3:30). True spiritual fathers will encourage their offspring to align with other father/mother gifts when doing so will benefit their future. I have a spiritual son and daughter who aligned with another apostolic father and mother with my blessing. I realized at the time that they needed more than I could give them as a father gift. They followed that route and today are doing amazing things for the glory of the Father. This shift in no way altered our relationship, and I continue to be a father gift to them. For them to be aligned with another father gift does not remove the love in our hearts for one another. Fathers are not entitled to be the sole influence in the lives of spiritual sons and daughters. True fathers freely release and empower all their sons and daughters to soar into their destinies. It is one of the marks of a successful relationship. It is part of the blessing of fatherhood.

Spiritual fathers and mothers must also deal with their own wounds with humility and intentionality. They must each be honest about their faults and recognize themselves as a work in progress. They must be careful not to become co-dependent upon their sons and daughters for emotional or natural support or allow their offspring to do the same with them. Seeking counsel is one thing; seeking permission and approval is another. True fathers will always leave important life decisions of the sons and daughters in their own hands. They will advise and offer counsel, but they will not maneuver and manipulate the decisions of their spiritual children, even if their decisions are perceived by the father to be wrong choices.

By the same token, spiritual sons and daughters should always honor and respect their spiritual parents out of love rather than duty or parental expectation. Spiritual sons and daughters have rights of sonship but should never demand those rights of their spiritual parents. They are to be received with love and grace and enjoyed as a blessing from the Father.

Remember, father-son and father-daughter relationships are ordained of God, not men. Father God must set the timing and manner in which these relationships are born. Whatever is born of the Spirit will last; that which is born of the flesh will self-destruct. The outcome of flesh-born relationships will only end in wounds, hurt, and bitterness from unmet expectations that fuel the orphan spirit. Spirit-born relationships will thrive in peace, prosperity, and the fruit of the Spirit.

Correction is an essential part of spiritual parenting, and how one does this is critical. Spiritual fathers and mothers are teachers who operate relationally in love. They may become annoyed or angry at certain times in the relationships with spiritual offspring; however, they do not confront their spiritual children in anger, angst, indignation, or shame. True spiritual fathers know they are far from perfect as well, and they will bring correction in a spirit of love and grace to redirect their spiritual offspring in a healthy and blessed manner.

We are in an era where the Father is raising up spiritual parents to steward the hearts of the generations. As spiritual parents, we are tasked with turning the hearts of an orphan generation to the Father of glory. We are to lay the foundation for many generations to walk upon and become the fathers and mothers of the faith for future generations.

Chapter 5: Understanding Spiritual Fatherhood Review

In Chapter 5, we took a deeper dive into spiritual fatherhood. We looked at life examples of how healthy, spiritual mature father/son relationships function.

Questions:

1. Have you had a spiritual father or mother in your walk of faith?
2. Is that spiritual parent in a continuous relationship with you or did it last for a season?
3. Describe how that relationship(s) impacted your life.
4. Why do you think we have spiritual parental relationships for seasons and others are long lasting?
5. If there was correction during this relationship, how was it given and how was it received?
6. How did you grow during this relationship?

6

The Spirit of Fatherhood

There is a fundamental truth that most all of us learned in our Bible training days. The Father, Son, and Holy Spirit speak from a common mind and common source. There are not three wills nor three minds of God. The Father is essentially one and manifestly Three. There is no division in the Godhead. The Father doesn't speak, and the Son shake His head as if to say, "The old guy just has it all wrong." Neither does the Holy Spirit listen to the Son and then determine to execute a third alternative to the directive He received. Jesus made it clear, *The words that I say to you I do not speak on My own initiative, but the Father abiding in Me does His works* (John 14:10 NASB). So, everything that the Holy Spirit says is said in complete harmony with Father and Son.

It is important to revisit what Jesus shared with his disciples before yielding to His destiny of being bruised, beaten, despised, rejected, and nailed to and crucified upon the cross of Calvary. Look at a few of His words:

John 14:15-18 (TPT) *Loving me empowers you to obey my commands. And I will ask the Father and he will give you another Savior, the Holy Spirit of truth, who will be to you a friend just like me – and he will never leave you ... you know him intimately because he remains with you and will live inside you. I promise that I will never leave you helpless or abandon you as orphans, I will come back to you!*

John 15:1-2 (TPT) *I am the true sprouting vine, and the farmer who tends the vine is my Father. He cares for the branches connected to me by lifting and propping up the fruitless branches and pruning every fruitful branch to yield a greater harvest.*

John 15:16 (TPT) *You didn't choose me, but I've chosen and commissioned you to go into the world to bear fruit. And your fruit will last, because whatever you ask of my Father, for my sake, he will give it to you! So, this is my parting commandment: Love one another deeply.*

The Holy Spirit is the Spirit of the Father and his Fatherhood. He lives within us. He props and holds us up when we are going through troubled, hard times in life. He prunes us to make us more fruitful (that is, just like Him). His love for us never wavers, and His heart for us never changes. We are never too ugly that He would reject us and never so wonderful that we could earn His favor.

Oneness with Father through the Son by the enablement of the Holy Spirit is the essence of our inheritance. Jesus further shared in John 16:13-15 (TPT) these words of life-changing truth:

But when the truth-giving Spirit comes, he will unveil the reality of every truth within you. He won't speak of himself, but only what he hears from the Father, and he will reveal prophetically to you what is to come. He will glorify me on the earth, for he will receive from me what is mine and reveal it to you. Everything that belongs to the Father belongs to me – that's why I say the Divine Encourager will receive what is mine and reveal it to you.

The Holy Spirit is the presence of the Father within you. He is eternal and makes His earth home in your spirit. You are His temple and His anointed sons and daughters. He is the Father of your spirit; and through your life, He affirms and manifests Himself through you to advance His kingdom agenda in the earth. Look at the truth that Paul shared in Romans 8:14-17 (TPT):

The mature children of God are those who are moved by the impulses of the Holy Spirit. And you did not receive the spirit of religious duty, leading you back into the fear of NEVER BEING GOOD ENOUGH. But you have received the Spirit of FULL ACCEPTANCE, enfolding you into the family of God. And you will NEVER FEEL ORPHANED, for as he rises up within us, our spirits join him in saying the words of tender affection, Beloved Father! For the Holy Spirit makes God's Fatherhood real to us as he whispers into our innermost being, You are God's beloved child! And since we are his true children, we QUALIFY to share his treasures, for indeed we are heirs of God Himself.

Paul further shared in Acts 17:28 (TPT), *It is through Him that we live and function and have our IDENTITY; just as your poets have said, Our lineage comes from Him.* The King James version says, *For we are His offspring!*

Father shares His heart with us through our spirit. We share His authority; that is, the ability to rule on His behalf in earth and the heavens. We share His trustworthiness, or His ability to hold confidence. We share his values to walk uprightly and honorably with one another. We share His affection in order to love as He loves. Furthermore, we share his faithfulness to believe what He says IS; and we share His acceptance in order to rest in His unfailing favor. Most of all, we share His love and healing to restore and renew our broken hearts.

As we grow in the truth of our sonship in Christ, we begin to grow and mature into the Spirit of His Fatherhood. John further records in 1 John 3:1-2 (TPT) *Look with wonder at the depths of the Father's marvelous love that he has lavished on us! He has CALLED us and MADE us His VERY OWN BELOVED CHILDREN ... Beloved, we are God's children right now; however, it is not yet apparent what we will become. But we do know that when it is finally made visible, WE WILL BE JUST LIKE HIM for we will SEE HIM AS HE TRULY IS.* The more that we grow and mature in our relationship with Father as sons and daughters, the more we will become like the FATHER HE IS! We will become the express image of the FATHER by HIS SPIRIT.

> He has sent His word and Spirit into the earth realm to nurture and to develop us into the spiritual fathers and mothers we are destined to become.

When I was a child, I wanted to be like my dad. I always felt safe when I was with him. If he was running an errand, I wanted to go with him. If he was going to hunt with his friends, I wanted to go too. We went to cattle auctions, and we checked on our cattle in the pasture together. He coached me in Little League baseball, and on occasion we fished. He owned a grocery business during my teenage and college years, and I looked forward to each opportunity I had to work alongside him in the store. I watched him and would do what he did; and I recall when assisting a customer one day, the customer commented, "Boy, you are just like your daddy!" The customer meant it as a compliment, and I received it as such. Dad encouraged me to complete my college education, and he supported me in my life endeavors until his untimely line of duty death as a law enforcement officer in 1984. It is incredibly painful to lose a father, but I treasure the memories of his life and hold to the life lessons that I learned from him.

In the early years of my nursing career, I served at the Dallas Veterans Administration Hospital as a research nurse under Dr. Thomas Smitherman. Dr. Smitherman was a cardiologist and professor at Southwestern Medical School in Dallas, and I truly admired this wonderful man.

He selected me to work with his team on an aspirin research study. The purpose of this study was to determine whether or not aspirin therapy could help reduce heart attacks. Today many of us take low dose (baby) aspirin to reduce the possibility of developing clots that can cause heart attacks.

Over the years that I served with Dr. Smitherman, I learned about the human heart and how diseases negatively affect its optimal function. He encouraged me to further my studies in nursing, and I completed my Master of Science in Nursing degree while serving with him. However, I learned much more than understanding the human heart; I also learned about the character and nature of Dr. Smitherman himself. He loved his family and was very dedicated to his life mission. However, he was also interested in the well-being of those of us who served with him. He treated us more like co-laborers than employees. He extended to us the greatest respect and encouraged us to excel in our life goals and dreams. His profession was to heal the human hearts of men, but he also modeled his father heart as a person to those of us around him.

The longer I served with Dr. Smitherman, the more I became like him in many ways. I began to view life like he did. I began to think somewhat like he did. His life values began to rub off on me, and I found myself often exhibiting some of his mannerisms, even at times walking like he did. It is fair to say that I truly loved this man, and

I continue to love and appreciate him today for all that he contributed to my life and future. I moved on after the aspirin study was completed and taught nursing for many years until the Father called me into full-time ministry.

In 2000, after eight years of ministry training in California, I returned to my home state in Texas to begin a life assignment from the Lord. Soon after returning, I was introduced to a man who became my spiritual father, Jim Hodges. Brother Jim and his wife Jean have been spiritual parents to me and my family. They adopted us, have loved and nurtured us, opened their ministry home to us, and have given us a seat at their table for more than 22 years. On more than one occasion Brother Jim has shared his spiritual mantle with me to accomplish spiritual matters that were above my pay grade. He has taught me about the kingdom of God and so many other things from scripture and life that have shaped my character as a follower of Jesus. He is an amazing role model of a genuine father heart for many of us who are under his spiritual covering. And would you believe, I often find myself thinking like him, talking like him, and exhibiting mannerisms like him.

There have been other father and mother gifts throughout stages in my life that I could share. From boyhood to now in my later years, each one was uniquely assigned by the Father to me for specific purposes in the growth and maturing process of my life. The point is this, in each of these relationships, I drew from the life of their spirits into my own life. The behaviors of these men that I exhibited were not intentional. They were not conscious efforts to be like someone else. These mannerisms were evidence of impartation into my spirit of what the Father had placed into their spirits from HIS Spirit. I was literally catching the spirit of these two men (and others in my life) that Father God had deposited within them. As I walked closely, heart to heart, with them; Father would release some of His virtue inside of them into me!

This is the biblical principle of spiritual impartation. We become like those with whom we associate. We draw from the spirits of others when we align our hearts with theirs. Whoever has your ear will also influence your heart and soul. This is why it is so critical to know those with whom you labor and to guard your heart with all diligence (Proverbs 4:23).

When Jesus called His disciples, His first words were, *Follow me* (Matthew 4:19). His earth mission was to reconnect mankind to His Father. He shared the truths about His Father with them and modeled the Father's heart for them. They walked with Him, slept with Him, ate meals with Him, and ultimately received the Spirit OF HIM. He sent them out to minister to others by healing the sick, cleansing the lepers, raising the dead, casting out demons, and declaring that the kingdom of heaven (The Father) had come (Matthew 10:8; Luke 10:9). When they returned and were ecstatic that demons were subject to them in the name of Jesus, Jesus responded, do not rejoice that demons are subject to you, but rejoice that your names are written in heaven (Luke 10:20). Our relationship with Father is greater than our anointing and gifting. From the heart of Father all things of heaven flow into the earth, bringing glory to whom it belongs—Father God!

Jesus trained his disciples to become sons who would grow and mature into the fathers of the faith that we know them to be today. When their training was completed through Jesus, the Father poured His Spirit out upon them on the Day of Pentecost for the Spirit to complete what Jesus began. He is doing the same with us today. He has sent His word and Spirit into the earth realm to nurture and to develop us into the spiritual fathers and mothers we are destined to become. The longer we live in the Spirit of the Son, the more be become like the Father who created ALL SONS.

We have not been baptized into the Holy Spirit of the Son to simply birth our ministries. We have not been given the rights of sonship and daughterhood to simply demand our birthright to launch our ministries or become miracle working gifts to the world. We have not been given access to the Throne Room of Father to have a special place of elitism as a five-fold minister. No, we have been invited and welcomed into the family of the Father as sons and daughters to become transformed into the very image and likeness of Father Himself. What an amazing and humbling honor this is—to be invited into His heart and mature into the express image and likeness of Father Himself. This is greater than becoming like my dad, Dr. Smitherman, or Brother Jim. This is the greatest and highest honor of all! When we see Him as He truly is, we will then see ourselves as we truly ARE.

I pray that you, the mature sons, daughters, mothers, and fathers of the faith will walk in His sevenfold Spirit (Isaiah 11:1-2), especially His wisdom and understanding. I pray that that you operate your life in synchrony with His, and that you would know His voice and feel His heartbeat in yours. I pray that you seek His abiding above His anointing. I challenge you to take stock in whom you are following and allowing to speak into your heart. Finally, I pray that you be blessed by the prayer of Paul in Ephesians 4:1-6 (TPT):

> When we see Him as He truly is, we will then see ourselves as we truly ARE.

As a prisoner of the Lord, I plead with you to walk holy, in a way that is suitable to your high rank given to you in our divine calling. With tender humility and quiet patience always demonstrate patience and generous love toward one another, especially toward those who may try our patience. Be faithful to guard the sweet harmony of the Holy Spirit among you in the bonds of peace, being one body and one spirit, as you were called into the same glorious hope of divine destiny. For the Lord is one, and so are we, for we share in one faith, one baptism, and one Father. And he is the PERFECT FATHER who leads us all, works through us all, and lives in us all.

Our highest call and destiny in this life is not to achieve great fame and notoriety as the men and women of God. Rather, it is to be continually transformed into the image and likeness of the PERFECT FATHER through the life of HIS SON and OUR BROTHER, Jesus, through the operation and guidance of Holy Spirit.

Chapter 6: The Spirit of Fatherhood Review

In Chapter 6, we discussed the spirit of fatherhood. Our highest call and destiny in this life is not to achieve great fame and notoriety as men and women of God, but to be continually transformed into the image and likeness of the Father through the life of Jesus and the guidance of Holy Spirit.

Questions:

1. Compare your current spiritual health to where you were five years or even 1 year ago. Has there been growth? Growth in what area?
2. As we mature as spiritual sons and daughters, we look for opportunities to parent the next generation. Do you have a spiritual son or daughter?
3. Are you now spiritually mature enough to parent a spiritual son or daughter? If not, when?
4. Just like parenting in the natural comes with great responsibility, spiritual fathers and mothers take on responsibility in that role. How do you feel about that?
5. Define the areas of where you need to spiritually mature before accepting a spiritual parent role. Pray and ask Holy Spirit to reveal any areas of your life where you need to change or mature to prepare you to parent the next generation.

7

A New Generation of Apostolic Fathers and Mothers

In Matthew 24:2 Jesus said to His disciples, *Truly I say to you, not one stone here will be left upon another, which will not be torn down* (NASB). This verse was a summation of what Jesus shared with his disciples on the Mount of Olives after declaring that the temple in Jerusalem would be completely destroyed. Upon hearing this declaration from Him, the disciples asked the logical question. When will this happen, and what signs shall we look for to signal your coming and the completion of this age?

Jesus answered their question throughout the verses that followed. He listed the signs to be 1) Deception would lead many away from truth through those claiming to be God's anointed, when in fact they were deceivers, 2) Hearing of wars and the rumors of wars nearby, and revolutions on every side causing panic and fear, and 3)

Breaking apart of the world's systems that are destined to occur (Matthew 24:4-6a). Jesus goes on to say that these events are just the beginning, and the end of this age will continue to unfold.

Jesus continued with more answers by declaring that 1) Nations going to war against each other and kingdoms warring against kingdoms, and 2) Terrible earthquakes, seismic events of epic proportion, epidemics, and famines in place after place. These would be the first contractions and birth pains of what the new age would look like in its beginning stages (Matthew 24:7-8). Jesus continued with other signs of the end of the age, including persecution, hatred, and death for followers of Christ because of their love for Him. Lying prophets would emerge and lead many from truth through their deceptions. Sin and lawlessness would increase among those whose hearts once burned for Jesus, and others will simply grow cold in their heart. (Matthew 24:9-12).

Jesus ends this harrowing account of events to come with hope. In Matthew 24:14, Jesus said, *Yet through it all, this joyful assurance of the realm of heaven's kingdom will be proclaimed all over the world, providing every nation with a demonstration of the reality of God, And after this the end will come.*

Scholars have debated these verses in the Bible for generations, so I do not propose to be an expert on the eschatological ramifications of this passage. However, I do know this. The destruction of Jerusalem and the temple occurred in A.D. 70, and the end of this age will one day close as well. The signs that Jesus shared on the Mount of Olives occurred before the fall of Jerusalem, and those same signs are manifesting in our day as well. The destruction of Jerusalem in AD 70 marked the official end of Judaism, and the end of this age will be marked by the return of Jesus.

The major question at hand for us today is: What are we doing to advance the Father's kingdom agenda in the earth in the meantime? Jesus said that we were to continue to proclaim the gospel of the kingdom to every nation. This is more than Sunday church; this is a lifestyle of imparting the truth and authority of the gospel into all areas of the culture. We, the sons and daughters and mothers and fathers of the faith must continue to proclaim and model the pattern of the kingdom in the earth as Genesis 1:28 stewards.

Paul shared with his sons and daughters in Rome, *Love obligates me to preach to everyone, to those who are among the elite and those who are among the outcasts, to those who are wise and educated as well as those who are foolish an unlearned* (Romans 1:14 TPT). No one modeled this better than Paul. As a father of the faith, he demonstrated to us how to get this done in our generation. The gospel of the kingdom of God is the proclamation of the dominion of King Jesus over everything, including all of heaven and earth. This means that His dominion will be demonstrated as a witness to all the nations of the earth. It further means that Jesus has the right of rulership, ownership, and

Lordship of all the nations of the earth. He is the King of heaven and the globe!

> **What are we doing to advance the Father's kingdom?**

Very few are not aware that we are living in the era of the Kingdom Movement. This era will not be completed until every knee bow and every tongue confesses that Jesus Christ is the true King of heaven and earth. This will not mean that all mankind will be born again, but it does mean that there will be a worldwide demonstration of Father's power and authority over the elements, people, death, and nature. This demonstration also includes an increase of apostolic and prophetic manifestations, signs and wonders, and miracles to the point that all will acknowledge that there is no true God but Jesus Christ.

This movement will also align with the words of the prophet Haggai. He prophesied, *For thus says the Lord of Hosts, once more in a little while I am going to shake the heavens and the earth, the sea also and the dry land. And I will shake all the nations; and they will come with the wealth of all nations; and I will fill this house with glory, says the Lord of hosts* (Haggai 2:6-7). As the Church progresses through the Kingdom Age, the sons and daughters of the faith will continue to preach the gospel with demonstrations of supernatural power until all nations turn to Jesus.

When Jesus taught his disciples to pray, he prayed to the Father, *Thy kingdom come, thy will be done on earth as it is in heaven* (Matthew 6:10 KJV). In this prayer, Jesus prayed for

His Father's kingdom to fully manifest in the earth realm. He was not asking the Father to consider this as a future option. He was declaring the day that this would be a reality. We are closing in on that day in this final Age of the Kingdom.

This is the time when the new generation of apostolic fathers and mothers must arise to steward the sons and daughters who will be used of the Father to bring this age into its fullness. It is not enough that we as the fathers and mothers of the faith be content to sit on the sidelines and watch these events unfold. We must actively engage in the lives of the emerging generations of sons and daughters and impart into them the wisdom and knowledge we have been given to model fatherhood such as Dr. Smitherman and Apostle Jim Hodges and others like them have done for my generation.

It begins in our realm of influence, whether it be in the small setting of our personal family, a larger setting of a small group or church family, or in a regional, national, or international arena. We must each find our specific place and engage the next generation of sons and daughters in the pursuit of their end-time destiny and life purpose. This is the mission for us as apostolic fathers and mothers. We must not miss our day of visitation and assignment. We must steward the coming generations to advance the kingdom of God at home and abroad.

> This is the time when the new generation of apostolic fathers and mothers must arise to steward the sons and daughters who will be used of the Father to bring this age into its fullness.

Recently I was in a season of prayer. During one of my prayer times, I was literally taken up in the Spirit and found myself standing before the Lord's presence. In this vision, the Lord had a set of ancient keys of different sizes in his hand. He took the largest key of the set and removed it from the keyring. He then extended his hand toward me and said, *This key is yours to use as often as you like.* As I gazed at the key, almost afraid to touch it much less take it from the Lord's hand, He said this to me. *This key is the Master Key. It is the key to my heart and unlocks all that is in my heart for you. As much and as often as you need or desire to use this key, it is yours to keep.* I reached my hand out and took the key from the Lord's hand, and in a prophetic act, I pointed the key toward Him and turned the key. Immediately, the love in the Lord's heart began to pour out into mine. It was so overwhelming that I crumpled in awe before Him and bathed in His wonderful, beautiful presence. I then looked at the key, and on the shaft of the key was inscribed the word, *Love.*

I knew the message to me in this vision was this: Love is the Master Key to the heart of the Father. His love is revealed to us and poured out upon us as often and as much as we can receive it. His love activates our hearts to beat one with His and to engage in the things of this life that are most near and dear to His own heart. May your heart also beat as one with His. May His love be poured out upon and into you to the point that you crumple before Him in awe and experience the depth of His love for you and all that He has created.

In Ephesians 3:14-19, Paul prayed, *So I kneel humbly in awe before the Father of our Lord Jesus Christ, the Messiah, the PERFECT FATHER of every father and child in heaven and on the earth. And I pray that he would unveil within you the unlimited riches of his glory and favor until supernatural strength floods your innermost being with His divine might and explosive power. Then, by constantly using your faith, the life of Christ will be released deep inside you, and the resting place of his love will become the very source and root of your life. Then you will be empowered to discover what every holy one experiences – the great magnitude of the astonishing love of Christ in all its dimensions. How deeply intimate and far-reaching is his love! How enduring and inclusive it is! Endless love beyond measurement that transcends our understanding – this extravagant love pours out into you until you are filled with the fullness of God!* (TPT).

Paul goes on to say in Ephesians 3:20-21, *Never doubt God's mighty power to work IN YOU and accomplish all this. He will achieve infinitely more than your greatest request, your most unbelievable dream, and exceed your wildest imagination! He will outdo them all, for His miraculous power constantly energizes you. Now we offer up to God all the glorious praise that rises from every church in every generation through Jesus Christ – and all that will be manifest through time and eternity. Amen!*

In the name and authority of Jesus Christ, as a son of God and father of the faith, I decree the following over you. I invite you to read them aloud. As you do, you will join the symphony of others reciting aloud with you.

I decree that you will heed the call of God upon your life and come into your place of maturity as a son/daughter of the Eternal Father.

I decree that you will pursue the Holy Spirit as He leads and guides you into the wisdom and understanding of your father/mother calling.

I decree that you will spiritually develop the sons and daughters that have been assigned and entrusted to your care.

I decree that you will walk in the full expression of the purposes and destiny of your life as the eternal offspring of your Father, God.

Now is the time for the new generation of apostolic fathers and mothers to arise! May the grace of our Lord Jesus Christ empower you to fulfill this mandate and assignment for this age. May His love engulf and infuse you to nurture, train, and impart the heart of the Father to the next generation of apostolic fathers and mothers.

7: A New Generation of Apostolic Fathers and Mothers Review

In Chapter 7, we challenged you to become the new generation of apostolic fathers and mothers to steward the sons and daughters who will be used of the Father to bring this age to its fullness.

Questions:

1. What are you doing to steward sons and daughters of the next generation?
2. What has God asked you to do that you are not doing? Why?
3. What will happen if you do not obey God and fulfill the calling of a spiritual father or mother to a son or daughter? What are the risks to you and your potential son or daughter?
4. Make a list of opportunities that are currently within your realm to influence the next generation. Ask Holy Spirit to prepare the way. Be an individual of action – activate the power within you!
5. Write the declarations on the previous page down, however replace "you" in the statements with your full name. I challenge you to read them out loud to yourself every day for the next 21 days. Journal the opportunities Holy Spirit brings to you. Share those experiences with others!

Biography

Larry Burden is an author, educator, businessman, and the founder of Kingdom Life International, Inc. For 20 years he served as Pastor of Kingdom Life Christian Center based in Frisco, Texas.

For more than 30 years, he has served in pastoral ministry, taught in international Bible colleges, ministered nationally and abroad, and served in various positions in the marketplace.

He also is an ordained senior chaplain with the International Fellowship of Chaplains where he serves as the Leadership Liaison, a chaplain trainer, and a member of the Board of Directors.

He also serves on the boards of the Federation of Ministries and Churches International under Apostle Jim Hodges and International Breakthrough Ministries under Apostle Barbara Wentroble.

Larry most recently established Kingdom Life Apostolic Ministries, through which he imparts and promotes the fatherhood of God throughout the nations.

Larry has been married to Kathy Burden for more than 48 years, and together, they have two sons and daughters-in-law and seven grandchildren.

Apostles Larry and Kathy work tirelessly to advance the Kingdom of God throughout the nations.

Made in the USA
Middletown, DE
25 November 2022

15832035R00060